DAVID HEALY

THE STORY SO FAR

First published in 2007 by
Appletree Press Ltd
The Old Potato Station
14 Howard Street South
Belfast BT7 1AP

Tel: +44 (0) 28 90 243074
Fax: +44 (0) 28 90 246756

Website: www.appletree.ie
Email: reception@appletree.ie

A catalogue record for this book is available from the British Library.

DAVID HEALY – THE STORY SO FAR

ISBN: 978 1 84758 047 4

Desk & Marketing Editor: Jean Brown
Editorial Work: Jim Black
Designer: Stuart Wilkinson
Production Manager: Paul McAvoy

9 8 7 6 5 4 3 2 1

AP3468

DAVID HEALY

THE STORY SO FAR

IVAN MARTIN

Appletree Press

HEALY

9

CONTENTS

" One of the things that makes David special is his attitude to the game. He still wants to learn. He is not one of those players who requires to be driven to be successful. David drives himself. As a finisher I would sum him up in one word – lethal! Quite simply, thats what he is all about. "

– Nigel Worthington

FOREWORD

David Healy is a Northern Ireland icon.

Yet writing a book about him is so different from the one I did about George Best in 2005. For a start Bestie's greatest moments came at club level. For Healy the greatest glory has come while wearing the green shirt of Northern Ireland. Sadly George died the year I wrote about him while David is currently in his prime. He is 28 years old, playing in the Premiership with Fulham, his international pedigree increasing with every goal.

George was the greatest player ever to come out of Northern Ireland. He was two-footed, a supreme dribbler, a goal-scorer and maker and possessed an athleticism and balance that any sportsman – or ballet dancer – would die for.

David's currency is goals. He has all the attributes that enable him to play at the top level for sure, but what makes him stand out from the crowd is not his all-round ability but his exceptional talent as a finisher.

He is not merely the best goal-scorer of his generation of Northern Ireland footballers. He is simply the best finisher of any generation who have worn the green jersey. That is not in dispute, because the reality is that the stats don't lie. The bottom line is that David Healy has scored more goals for Northern Ireland than any other player living or dead. That is beyond dispute. It is a hard fact in the same way as there are 12 inches in a foot; babies cry when they are hungry; or Jose Mourinho is not on Roman Abramovich's Christmas card list!

Healy's goal-scoring exploits for his country are second-to-none. But he will always be revered for 'that goal' against England at Windsor Park in September 2005. With 74 minutes of the match gone it remained scoreless. Healy, who had been operating all evening on that thin line between off-side and on-side, made another run. Steve Davis delivered a perfectly weighted pass. Healy was on to it in a flash, and with the wretched Rio Ferdinand and the stranded Ashley Cole screaming for an off-side decision, he bore in on Paul Robinson.

As Windsor Park held its breath the kid from Killyleagh, already his country's leading scorer with 18 goals, moved forward, took aim and shot. Paul Robinson in the England goal could only look on despairingly as the ball flew past him into the net. The stadium erupted, the players celebrated. It has even been alleged that Lawrie Sanchez smiled!

Right: So what was the secret of Northern Ireland's success that memorable night in September 2005? The players were to subsequently reveal that the game plan was not to allow England time to settle on the ball, and to make Rio Ferdinand head it as often as possible. The Manchester United number 5, pictured here jostling with Healy, likes to get the ball down and play, with heading a necessary evil rather than a preferred option. The pleasing thing for Northern Ireland was that they played against an England team full of stars. This was no makeshift outfit. Steven Gerrard, Michael Owen, Frank Lampard, Joe Cole and Wayne Rooney were all there alongside skipper David Beckham and Ferdinand. Some of them could not believe it had happened afterwards, but it had. The team they had toyed with in a 4-0 win at Old Trafford had turned the tables. It was Lawrie Sanchez's finest hour in a fruitful spell as Northern Ireland manager.

England's defeated side were no park bench outfit either. It is not as if they fielded a bunch of rookies or took the opportunity to blood some of their perceived stars of the future. Premiership gladiators like Ferdinand, Cole, Stevie Gerrard, Wayne Rooney, Frank Lampard, John Terry were all aboard. Not to mention La Liga's finest at the time, David Beckham. The England team would return home with their tails between their legs for the first time since 1927.

This Northern Ireland team would go down in history. Healy's life would never be the same again. Just as Geoff Hurst's hat trick at Wembley in 1966 is the most enduring memory of that oft-mentioned World Cup win by England. Just as George Best's mazy dribble and confident, almost casual finish is the defining memory of Manchester United's European Cup win on 29 May 1968, so it was with David following that memorable goal against England. Northern Ireland had a new icon.

'King David' Healy will be forever remembered as that dragon who turned the tables on St George. He put Sven-Göran Eriksson's team to the sword and emerged as his country's knight in shining armour.

Overnight Healy moved from the back to the front pages of the newspapers. He was now a *bona fide* soccer legend. Proof, as if any were needed, soon surfaced when he began to be included in the murals which bedeck the walls of many of the working class hotbeds of Northern Ireland football.

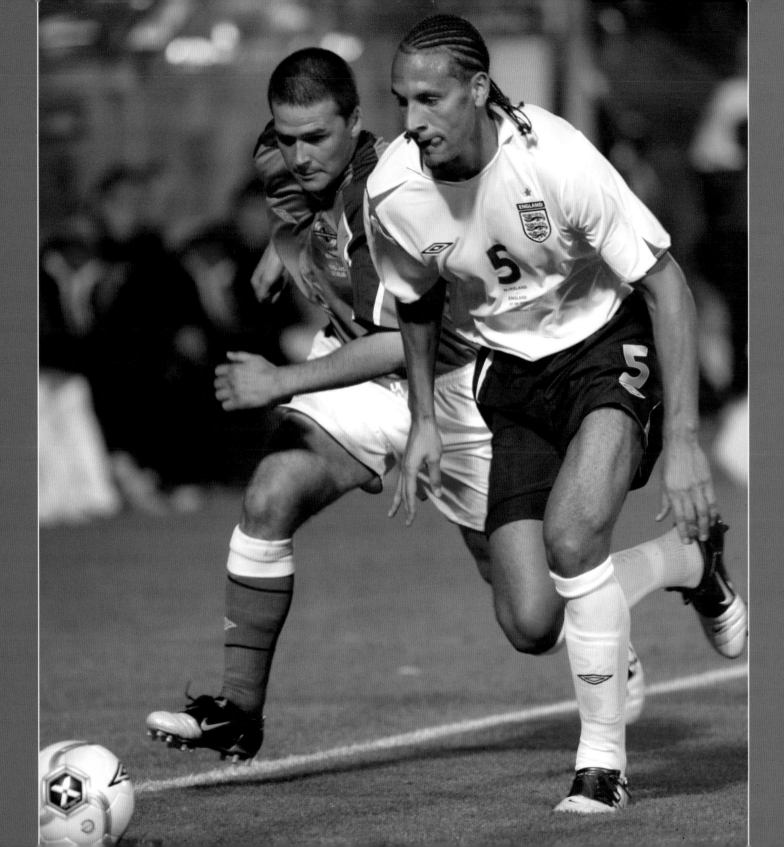

He was up there with the Danny Blanchflowers, the Pat Jennings and the greatest of them all, the incomparable Best. Exalted company perhaps, but none of those who already enjoyed iconic status could have failed to be impressed by Healy's goal-scoring prowess.

Dr Malcolm Brodie, who has seen it all in over half a century of reporting on Northern Ireland's games, is better placed than anyone to contextualise Healy's worth. "He is the best finisher Northern Ireland has ever had," purrs the man known as the doyen of football journalism in Northern Ireland.

But then he just carries on proving Malcolm's very valid point. For example he is the only player ever to have scored two hat-tricks for Northern Ireland. These came during his phenomenal run of goals in the Euro 2008 qualifiers. The first being against Spain at Windsor Park in September 2006, the second coming against Liechtenstein the following March.

Of the two hat-tricks, the three goals he bagged against Spain have to be the more impressive. Indeed I would go as far as to suggest that they even eclipse that memorable goal against England. The reason that I feel that to be the case is that in the game with Spain, Northern Ireland twice came from behind to chalk up a splendid 3-2 victory.

The match with Spain also came at a time when Northern Ireland were fighting to keep their Euro 2008 qualifying hopes alive after that sickening 3-0 home defeat by Iceland. It was a pressure situation. A must-win game. Whereas the England game came at a time when Northern Ireland's hopes of going to the 2006 World Cup had long since disappeared.

In the cold light of day you would have to own up to the fact that, delightful as it was to beat England, the joy was confined to that one evening. The feeling of exuberance and euphoria made the walk from the stadium to the Lisburn Road feel like a magic carpet ride. The only other sporting occasion I can compare it to which generated such uncontained joy was the evening at Loftus Road when Barry McGuigan defeated Eusebio Pedroza to lift the world featherweight title.

However even taking all that into account, I would still suggest that Healy's hat-trick against a talented Spanish side, packed with multi-million pound stars from Real Madrid and Barcelona, was, in pure football terms, a greater achievement. In truth both were unforgettable evenings. Healy himself would tend to be of the opinion that all the goals he scores bring him joy. The tap-ins and the scrappy ones meaning just as much as the quality finishes such as the one he fired past Peter 'The Great Dane' Schmeichel or indeed that superb lob against Spain for the winner and the hat-trick.

Left: David celebrates his hat-trick goal against Liechtenstein with Keith Gillespie

While that treble against Spain may well be the highlight of Healy's haul for Northern Ireland, his very first appearance for his country alerted the football public here to the fact that he was going to be special.

He was given his debut in an away game against Luxembourg by Sammy McIlroy. The 1982 World Cup hero had heard of "little David" as he usually referred to him, through his still strong connections with Manchester United. His decision to elevate the Under-21 international to the full squad raised a few eyebrows. It was a long way from Manchester United reserves to the international stage. But Sammy was convinced. He also knew that Healy's track record with the Under 21 side was good. He returned a goal every other game in his eight appearances.

So to the friendly with Luxembourg. Not only was it David's debut it was also Sammy Mac's first game in charge. He was not left long to wonder about his decision to select the Man Utd rookie.

Keith Gillespie, who was to become a rich source in terms of providing the ammunition for the man who would be King, picked Healy out with a pinpoint cross. It gave him his first international goal, albeit a confidence boosting tap-in. He then became the first player to bag a brace on his debut since Trevor Anderson in 1973, when he scored a second from Mark William's pass after 48 minutes.

Healy was up and running. Sammy McIlroy had his first win as an international manager. It was real 'Boys Own' stuff. Indeed David went on to score eight goals in the next eighteen months. But there was trouble ahead. Northern Ireland – and Healy – were to suffer a goal drought which went on for 1298 minutes and almost 28 months.

In some ways it has made the good times even better for Healy. He remembers the frustrations of those days, especially when some people were suggesting he should be dropped. "They were saying I couldn't hit a barn door," recalled the man who would ultimately smash the Northern Ireland all-time scoring record.

But when the duck was broken, after Sammy McIlroy had departed with Lawrie Sanchez replacing him, it was inevitable that Healy would score the goal against Norway. Once more Gillespie was the provider. Eleven minutes into the second half he slung over a cross, Healy got his head to it and it nestled in the net.

The 11,288 members of the green and white army breathed a collective sigh of relief and the Healy scoring show was on the road again. The fact that Northern Ireland lost 4-1 on the night is one of those facts lost forever in the mists of time. Who cared?

The new manager's tactics suited Healy. He was given a partner up-front, a luxury he seldom enjoyed under the previous incumbent. The goals kept coming and he equalled Billy Gillespie and Colin Clarke's Northern Ireland scoring record of 13 goals against Trinadad & Tobago with a cheeky 40-yard lob when there was confusion over who was getting a free-kick. It was his 35th appearance for his country. Then things got even better when he scored a second goal to become the all-time Northern Ireland top scorer with 14 goals. It was also the first time since his debut four years previously that he had scored two goals in an international match.

His next goal for his country was one few people will forget. It was scored in a tense World Cup qualifier with Wales in the cauldron-like atmosphere of the Millennium Stadium in Cardiff. David lobbed the Welsh keeper Paul Jones to put ten-man Northern Ireland (Michael Hughes and Robbie Savage having taken very early baths) 2-0 up. However the Italian referee decided the Preston striker's celebrations were too enthusiastic and produced a red card. It instantly ruled Healy out of the next international with Azerbaijan. He returned the following month against Austria and scored a spectacular goal. Normal service had been resumed. The England match at Windsor Park came three games later and since then David has become the talisman of the Northern Ireland team.

This book traces his journey from Killyleagh to the Premiership. It is a pictorial record of his career to date. Obviously his Northern Ireland success dominates but we also chart his club career. That began at Lisburn Youth and on to Manchester United when David was still a slip of a schoolboy from Killyleagh in Co. Down.

After his trainee days at Old Trafford where he made three senior appearances, David had a spell at Port Vale before signing for David Moyes at Preston North End. He enjoyed a fruitful time there,

scoring 45 goals in 157 appearances. He flirted with a move to Norwich City, managed at the time by Nigel Worthington, before moving from Lancashire to Yorkshire instead and joining Leeds United. His hopes of achieving Premiership football with the financially challenged Elland Road club, whose fall from the big time has been one of the most spectacular in modern football, never got past first base.

But it was inevitable that someone with David's proven record at the highest level would become a target for a top-flight club. His desire for Premiership football finally came to pass in the summer of 2007 when he joined Fulham.

His challenge now is to try and replicate his exceptional Northern Ireland goal-scoring record at club level. His success in meeting that challenge could ultimately determine whether or not Fulham continue in the top flight.

It will be one of the most intriguing aspects of the 2007–08 season.

Ivan Martin

THE STORY SO FAR

Left: Even record-breaking international superstar goal-scorers have to start somewhere. With David it was with his village team in Killyleagh and then on to Lisburn Youth. He may have been small but that did not prevent his goal-scoring prowess from shining through. Soon he caught the eye of a Manchester United scout. In Manchester they had plenty of previous experience of scrawny kids coming to the club. Norman Whiteside was an obvious exception as he was already around six feet tall at 14 years of age. But everyone at the club well remembered a young teenager who came from Northern Ireland called George Best. He too was tiny. But by the time he was playing in the first team at United he could easily have been the tallest man in the world, if he had been able to stand on his reputation!

Above: David has admitted that one of the great things about going to Manchester United while still a child was getting to meet your heroes. Although still some years away from his knighthood when this picture was taken, the then-Alex Ferguson was already royalty to everyone associated with the Old Trafford club. So imagine the thrill it must have been for the young Healy to have this picture taken with the man known to the red half of Manchester as simply 'The Boss'. David has often remarked how Ferguson went out of his way to make him and his parents feel special any time they were over at Old Trafford, before he committed himself to the club on leaving school. He also revealed that he sought and got Ferguson's advice when he felt he needed to move on, to enhance his fledgling international career with regular first team football.

Above: This is a sight that Northern Ireland fans have come to know and love! David Healy turns away after scoring in a World Cup qualifier against Denmark back in 2000. It was the little striker's second goal for his country in front of the Windsor Park faithful. It was also the first time he had scored for his country in a competitive game. But when this game was played any talk of Healy going on to more than double the all-time scoring record for Northern Ireland was all in the future. The interesting thing about this game was that Healy had rattled his goal past the former Manchester United custodian Peter Schmeichel. Before the game 'the Great Dane' had indicated that he did not know anything about his former Old Trafford colleague. But when the Killyleagh kid blasted a 25-yard effort past him it was unlikely that Schmeichel would ever forget him again. The game finished 1-1.

Right: This picture is taken from the World Cup qualifier against Denmark in which David ensured that Peter Schmeichel would never again be in any doubt as to who he is! The Danes had arrived in Belfast with an experienced side, notably their blond keeper who was winning his 127th cap. Other household names included Jon Dahl Tomasson, Jesper Gronkjaer and the two Thomases, Helvig and Gravesen. Once Healy, playing as a lone striker, identified himself as the danger man he came in for some rough treatment from the visitors. Gravesen in particular made his presence felt. Our picture shows him backing into Healy. However that was mild compared to a high and nasty tackle just before half-time which incensed the home crowd. Sadly for Northern Ireland Dennis Rommedahl equalised Healy's opener on the hour mark. After that the Danes created the better of the chances but the boys in green, inspired at the back by the resolute Gerry Taggart, held out. Healy's first competitive goal was his fifth in six games for his country.

Left: Sir Alex Ferguson has recently admitted that reserve team football in England is virtually a youth league. It is a place where young players who are 'so near yet so far' from the first team squad play their football. David is pictured here with two United legends Paul Scholes and the man voted best Premiership player ever Roy Keane, playing against Ipswich Town on 23rd December 2000, aged 21. He had begun travelling to Manchester at around 12 years of age. When he went there he was the latest in a long line of players from Northern Ireland dreaming of becoming a United legend. While he never reached the heights at Old Trafford of fellow countrymen like Sammy McIlroy – ironically the man who first capped him for Northern Ireland, Norman Whiteside, who remains the youngest player to appear in a World Cup or the greatest of them all George Best, Healy the hitman has no regrets. He always remembers the welcome he got there as a young man. He cherishes the fact that he met his heroes and was accepted by them. But most of all he treasures the welcome extended to his parents. He also benefited from being brought up on the good habits, both as a footballer and a person, which United try to instil in the youngsters in their charge. David Healy may not have fulfilled his ultimate dream at Manchester United but he has absolutely no regrets about having been there. Nor does he feel he got a raw deal. "It is every kid's dream to play for Manchester United," reasons Northern Ireland's all-time leading scorer. "Very few get the chance. But I did. It doesn't matter whether you played for United three times or three hundred times: you can always say that you did it."

Above: When David trotted out as a substitute in a game against Ipswich Town at Old Trafford before a packed Old Trafford on 23 December 2000 it was the best early Christmas present he had ever received. Here he is going up for the ball against Ipswich Town's John McGreal. Ten weeks earlier he had shocked Peter Schmeichel and Denmark at Windsor with what has since often been described as the best of his glut of goals for Northern Ireland. Now David was following in his footsteps in the red of Manchester United but the pair were not destined to be team mates though, as the 'Great Dane' had left for Sporting Lisbon the previous year. All too soon, just six days later in fact, Healy was also using the Old Trafford exit door for the next phase of his career at Preston. The previous February he had been allowed to go on loan to Port Vale to give him more competitive football than he was getting in the United reserve team. He played 16 matches for the club and scored three goals before returning to Old Trafford. Six days after featuring in the game with Ipswich David was allowed to go to Preston on loan. It was the beginning of the end of his time in Manchester. Within a week Preston had agreed a £1.5 million fee with United and the Northern Ireland international moved to Deepdale. "It was the right thing to do at the time" explains David. "Despite playing against Ipswich, I knew that I was maybe fifth or sixth in the pecking order of strikers at United. To allow my international career to continue I needed to be playing first team football and Preston were offering that."

Above: In March 2001 Northern Ireland played the Czech Republic in a World Cup qualifier. The Czechs were rated the sixth-best side in the world at that time. But instead of the build-up being about a possible David and Goliath struggle at Windsor Park it was overshadowed by events at a previous game in Belfast which had shamed Northern Ireland football. Neil Lennon was playing his club football at the time in Glasgow for Celtic. A section of the home support booed Lennon every time he touched the ball throughout the match. The IFA were incensed. They employed a private security firm to mingle with the crowd and identify anyone guilty of sectarian behaviour or verbal abuse. They also issued ten thousand red cards carrying the message 'Give Sectarianism The Boot'. The eyes of the world was on Northern Ireland football. The then-international manager Sammy McIlroy protected Lennon from the media glare in the build-up to the game. But the whole situation left him feeling very uncomfortable. It was a sideshow he could have done without. "You can't let a minority of people pick your team for you," rapped a defiant Sammy. David is pictured lining up for the national anthems before kick-off. In the event the Czech Republic won 1-0, propriety regarding Lennon aside, and now the clock was ticking on the Celtic midfielder's international career.

Above: While David's goal-scoring record at club level has never matched his headline-grabbing exploits for Northern Ireland, he will always be a striker who will score goals wherever he goes. He scored Preston's opening goal against Nottingham Forest during April 2001. This was his fourth month at the club after agreeing to join them on a permanent basis from Manchester United the previous January. Here David is being challenged during the match by Nottingham Forest's Chris Doig. This game was a vital one as both clubs were chasing a promotion play-off place. Healy settled North End's nerves by scoring after just 10 minutes. He was fouled just outside the box and stepped up to rifle the resulting free kick past Dave Beasant the Forest keeper. The pair were reunited some years later when Beasant was part of the coaching staff with the Northern Ireland team. Sadly David's goal did not prove to be the winner that day. Jon Olav Hjelde's injury-time equaliser left the spoils shared in a 1-1 draw. Preston's disappointment at failing to get promotion in Healy's first season faded in the close season as such things tend to do. By the start of the 2001–02 season the club were once more optimistic about making it to the top flight and joining their old rivals Bolton Wanderers who had pipped them the previous season.

Right: This picture features David playing for Preston North End in a match against Ipswich Town in September 2002. Both sides had made a decent start to the season and Preston, by now managed by the former Scotland supremo Craig Brown, were anxious to extend their unbeaten record. They managed to do that, but not in the way either Healy or Brown would have liked as the match finished scoreless. David was unlucky to see a well-struck effort in the second half kept out by the brilliance of Andy Marshall in the visitors' goal. Another Irish international player in the match but this time from south of the Border was Matt Holland who was playing for Ipswich Town. Holland, like David, was also out of luck that day when he saw his scoring effort crash off the crossbar and bounce to safety. Pulling the strings for Ipswich in midfield was Healy's Northern Ireland colleague Jim Magilton, who went on to become manager of the Tractor Men after hanging up his boots.

Right: This picture of David was taken during Northern Ireland's 2002 European Championship qualifying campaign. He is seen challenging Ukraine keeper Vitaliy Reva. Sadly that was about as challenging as it got for the Ukranian custodian as Northern Ireland failed to win for the sixth game running. Worryingly they also failed to score for the fifth international in a row. That barren sequence continued for a further 22 months and 13 games. Apart from an early effort by Healy and a header by George McCartney from a Michael Hughes cross, Northern Ireland were on the back foot for most of the game. Sergei Rebrov missed the visitors' best chance, and Andriy Voronin twice went close. Thank goodness there was no Andrei Shevchenko – who at that stage was plying his trade in Italy and rated the best striker in the world. These days both Healy and Shevchenko play in London, with life in the Premiership proving somewhat kinder to David than to the erstwhile goal-machine from Ukraine.

Left: In February 2003 Northern Ireland were in a downward spiral. Results had not been going their way. The last win the team had recorded had been at home to Malta in October 2001. The six games in the interim had yielded three defeats and three draws. The worrying thing was that apart from a 4-1 defeat by Poland, no goals had been scored. This did not improve against Finland who won 1-0 at Windsor Park on a foggy February evening. The hero for the Finns was winning his 50th cap and spoke English with a broad Scouse accent. The only goal of the game came from Liverpool skipper Sami Hyypiä, whose blond head proved to be a beacon in the gathering mire. At one point the referee feared that he might be forced to abandon the match. However in the event the introduction of an orange ball solved the problem. Hyypiä is amongst a posse of Finnish players closing in on Healy in our picture. On this occasion Healy was not designated the 'lone ranger' role and had James Quinn and then Andy Kirk as frontline partners. In the event the closest Northern Ireland came to scoring was when first Steve Lomas and late in the game Stuart Elliott headed against the woodwork. No joy in front of goal was to be the norm for Sammy McIlroy's team for some time to come.

Above: The look of frustration on David Healy's face says it all. Northern Ireland played Spain at home to Spain in the Euro 2004 qualifiers. Some positives to be taken were that they had not lost and they had kept a clean sheet. The jinx of June internationals, which had dogged the boys in green down the years, had not come to pass. This result had also ended a four game losing streak. That was the good news. The bad news was that once again Northern Ireland had failed to score. The draw with Spain was the tenth game in a row where that had happened. Healy was suffering more than most. Chances were proving few and far between, and he often found himself playing alone up front. The goal famine had become the main talking point before and after Northern Ireland games. It would continue for another eight months and thirteen internationals in total before it was ended, inevitably by one David Healy. When he rose to head Keith Gillespie's cross into the net in a friendly against Norway in February 2004 the relief at Windsor Park was such you could almost touch it.

DAVID HEALY

Left: This is a picture from the bad old days of David's international career. It comes from a European Championship qualifier against Greece in Belfast on 2 April 2003. The hard-running Healy is seen here pulling away from his marker Giorgios Karagounis. But it was to prove another disappointing afternoon as the visitors won 2-0. To make matters worse, a mere 7,187 hardy souls attended the game. The green and white army was in danger of becoming a mere platoon. Lack of goals was no help either. The match with the Greeks was followed in June by a defeat in Italy by a similar score and then a hugely credible scoreless draw in Spain. Was the tide starting to turn? Would that elusive goal come in the next game with Ukraine? Sadly not. There were no goals throughout the Euro 2004 qualifying campaign. Northern Ireland finished bottom of Group 6. On the plus side they conceded just eight goals in eight qualifying games. The big minus, of course, was that they did not score any themselves. Their lack of goals was becoming an international talking point. By the end of that campaign the side had not scored since February 2002, when Steve Lomas netted against Poland. The drought would ultimately last two years and five days as Northern Ireland went 1,298 minutes without a goal. It was a record for a European side and one nobody wanted.

Above: Just when everybody in the Northern Ireland camp thought things had bottomed out, the final home game of the Euro 2004 qualifying proved them wrong. It was 10 September 2003 when Armenia came to Belfast. Surely this was the game when Northern Ireland could get their first win of the campaign, and better still score a goal and "get that monkey off our backs," to quote Sammy McIlroy. Sadly nobody had told the Armenians, and they defeated a nervous home side who were almost trying too hard. That 1-0 home defeat hurt McIlroy badly. Not least because he had watched his team squander a plethora of chances. "I would love to know what more we have to do to score a goal," he sighed after the match. "The lads were all up for it but the ball just would not go into the net."

Left: With a goal-scoring record for Northern Ireland of better than a goal every two games who would have imagined that David would have a barren spell? But he would go 1,330 minutes between scoring in Malta in October 2001and triggering the biggest sigh of relief that has ever emanated from Windsor Park on 18 February 2004. Norway provided the opposition and Healy headed home Keith Gillespie's cross after 11 minutes of the second half. It was the first Northern Ireland goal since Steve Lomas had netted against Poland just over two years before. The famine had left the players' confidence at an all-time low. They just did not know where the next goal was coming from. So when it arrived some 1,298 minutes after its predecessor it was not just welcome but so special that the fact the Norwegians won the game 4-1 seemed irrelevant. The show was on the road again and within five games David had claimed the Northern Ireland goal-scoring record outright when his double against Trinidad & Tobago brought his total to 14.

Above: When Northern Ireland trotted out to face Norway on 18 February 2004 the team was at rock bottom. It had been over 1,200 minutes since a goal had gone in. Even Healy was under pressure. He winces when he remembers those days. Every player had his critics and some were suggesting he should not be in the team. He remembers one suggesting that he could not hit a barn door. To be fair to him the system of five in midfield and a lone striker, so often employed by Sammy McIlroy, did him no favours at all. As he has shown time after time in a green jersey, Healy needs decent service and a partner up front. When he gets that he can be deadly. This game was the first for Lawrie Sanchez as manager. While it may have been a bad time for the players there could not have been a better time for any new manager to come in. Northern Ireland could only go one way. Upwards. In the bland fashion that was to become his trademark the new manager revealed he had three aims. To get a goal. To get a win. To move up the FIFA rankings. Healy, seen here celebrating with Andy Smith, gave him the first with his 9th international goal. He gave him the second the following month with the winner in a 1-0 victory over Estonia. The rise up the FIFA rankings inevitably followed. That must have triggered a rare smile from the manager who, it is alleged, had negotiated a bonus of £1000 per FIFA ranking place.

Left: This picture was taken during David's time at Preston North End to give the club its full title, a throwback to the cloth cap days when they were the biggest club in Lancashire. The occasion was a pre-season friendly against county rivals Blackburn Rovers, another club with a long history in the game. Despite some decent early efforts by Healy the visitors were to be the winners, courtesy of a single goal by Paul Dickov. As ever at this stage of the season hopes were high, the pitches were like billiard tables and fans and players alike believed it was to be their season. Sadly that proved not to be the case and within three months David's career at Deepdale was over. The Northern Ireland striker moved to Leeds United, once a giant of a club who were hoping to recapture the glory days. His move to Leeds never brought his dream of Premiership football any closer, even though he did finish top scorer at the club that first season.

Above: This picture shows a bemused David Healy after he had been sent off by referee Domenico Messina in front of a 63,500 crowd at the Millennium Stadium in Cardiff. Northern Ireland were playing Wales in a World Cup qualifier in September 2004. It turned out to be one of those extraordinary nights that football is capable of conjuring up. The drama began after just eight minutes, when the Italian referee sent off Michael Hughes and Robbie Savage of Wales. But the Welsh, well ahead of Northern Ireland in the FIFA rankings and managed at the time by Mark Hughes, were firm favourites. Then Jeff Whitley pricked their balloon with a right-footed screamer from outside the box which left Paul Jones in the Welsh goal for dead. Healy added a second early in the second half and wheeled away in joy. The referee felt his celebrations were sufficiently over-the-top to give him a second yellow card, and he was off for an early bath. David later revealed that he was merely signalling in triumph to his father Clifford whom he knew to be in the stand he was looking up at. The goal stood. David walked. The Welsh dragged it back to 2-2 with goals from John Hartson and Rob Earnshaw.

Above: Following his dismissal against Wales David missed the international against Azerbaijan, but he was back in his beloved green jersey for the World Cup qualifier with Austria at Windsor Park the following October. As well as being back in the side he was soon back in the groove when he scored after 35 minutes. It was no ordinary goal either. This was a David Healy special. He picked up a short pass from Jeff Whitley 25 yards out, flicked it up, swivelled and rocketed what is known in the game as a 'pearler' past the astonished former Arsenal keeper Alex Manninger. The match finished 3-3 and an interested spectator was the then-Leeds United manager Kevin Blackwell. The Yorkshire club had been trailing Healy since the previous summer. Blackwell obviously needed no further convincing, and after a bit of haggling between Preston and Leeds, David duly moved to Elland Road a couple of weeks later.

Right: Despite enjoying his time – and a fair bit of success – at Preston David moved to Leeds simply because they were a big club. Despite an astonishing fall from grace, changes of ownership and the threat of bankruptcy they remained one of the best-supported teams in the country. Their opponents in this Coca-Cola League game were Burnley. David is pictured with the Clarets' James O'Connor. Amazingly this run-of-the-mill league game in chilly November attracted a crowd of 27,490, underlining Healy's belief that he had joined a big club, albeit a sleeping giant. Despite taking an early lead through Jermaine Wright with Healy and strike partner the beanpole Brian Deane involved in the build-up, Leeds lost 2-1. This was his second game in the white jersey of the Yorkshire outfit and two home defeats and no goals was hardly a fairytale start. But it was third time lucky for David in his next game when he bagged a brace in a 4-2 victory. Ironically Leeds' opponents that day were Preston, with Healy enjoying many happy returns to Deepdale with those two goals.

Right: If David Healy will never be allowed to forget 'that goal' at Windsor Park against England on 7 September 2005, his memories of the earlier away game with England in the same qualifying series will be entirely less pleasant. That game against England at Old Trafford the previous March indicated that with Northern Ireland life, as Ronan Keating's hit song put it, is a rollercoaster and you've got to ride it. The guys in green were trounced 4-0 by England whose coach Sven-Göran Eriksson was in charge that day for the fiftieth time. Amazingly Northern Ireland kept the game scoreless until two minutes after the interval. Three goals in six minutes from Joe Cole, Michael Owen and an own-goal by Chris Baird had the Lawrie Sanchez side reeling. When Frank Lampard, pictured here with Healy, added the fourth with 28 minutes left, Northern Ireland supporters feared complete embarrassment. But damage limitation became the order of the day and it stayed 4-0. This may have been the biggest defeat in Sanchez's time as manager but it was not the most embarrassing. That was a 1-0 home reversal against Canada which triggered a run of four straight defeats.

Left: This game with Germany was a friendly to celebrate the 125th anniversary of the Irish Football Association. It was organised through the then-IFA President Jim Boyce's network of contacts at the highest level around Europe, with the German team providing suitably prestigious opposition for such an auspicious occasion. After surviving some early German pressure Steve Davis' left wing cross was met by Keith Gillespie who rattled it towards goal. He seemed certain to score with Jens Lehmann beaten. Then Robert Huth dived to push it over the bar. He received an automatic red card and up stepped Healy to take the penalty. He slotted it home confidently, sending Lehmann the wrong way in the process. Sadly the joy of the supporters was short-lived. Even with ten men the Germans turned on the power and the style to run out 4-1 winners on the night. Hardly the happiest of anniversaries.

Above: Stuart Elliott is known for always running in on the keeper as soon as a penalty is struck. His rationale is simple. If the keeper saves the spot kick but fails to hold it, then a simple tap in is often on offer. On this occasion the Arsenal goalkeeper Jens Lehmann never got near it. Healy spun away in triumph and the first player to get to him to join in the celebrations was Elliott. It was David's 17th international goal and his third penalty for his country. Sadly the match went pear-shaped for Northern Ireland after that. The Germans equalised almost immediately. A defensive mistake allowed Gerald Asamoah to chest down a Michael Ballack cross and fire past Maik Taylor, who was born in Germany when his father was part of the British Army garrison. Ballack then turned goal taker, scoring twice, the second being a penalty before Lukas Podolski made it four. From a Northern Ireland point of view Michael Ingham, who replaced Taylor between the sticks and Gareth McAuley got some game time. It was the first occasion either had featured for the senior Northern Ireland side.

Right: David is pictured after scoring one of two goals against Millwall in a Coca-Cola championship game at Elland Road on the first day of the 2005–06 season. The game was played before a crowd of 20,440, a figure several Premiership clubs today would die for, but disappointing for Leeds' first game of the season. There were however extenuating circumstances. Firstly the game was live on Sky and more importantly Millwall had declined to take any ticket allocation for the match, because of a history of trouble between rival fans during and after this fixture. In the end Leeds won 2-1 with Healy grabbing both goals. The opener came after 28 minutes from open play while the second was a penalty. The victory got Leeds and David's season off to a flying start. Indeed it extended the Yorkshire club's record of not having been beaten in their opening day fixture to sixteen years. Healy's next goal for Leeds did not come for over a month, when he again bagged a brace in an exciting 3-3 draw at home to Brighton. However his opening day double was not the only time he scored during August. On a trip to Malta with Northern Ireland he had headed his side's only goal in a disappointing 1-1 draw.

Left: David is pictured here with the man who made that same lonely journey from his home in Northern Ireland to become an apprentice at Manchester United. George Best was a child of the swinging '60s. Indeed for many football people George Best *was* the swinging '60s! Some thirty-five years later when David went to United the club had learnt a lot. George was never shielded from the more excessive elements of the media in Manchester and beyond the way today's stars are. Take Ryan Giggs for example. He was never made available to the media until he was past his mid-twenties. When 'Fergie' says you talk you talk – and not a minute before! So David entered a world where it was already custom and practice that young players were protected, and where they were also encouraged to continue their education. This shot shows two Northern Ireland football legends of different generations rubbing shoulders, looking almost like father and son. Since George's untimely death David has helped keep his memory alive by doing some work for the George Best Memorial Trust. It was set up by the Best family to raise funds for research into alcohol-related problems and also to provide specialist coaching opportunities for young footballers. He has described his work with the Trust as "an honour and a privilege".

Above: This picture sees David relaxing at the team hotel ahead of the international friendly fixture in Malta in August 2005. The trip to the sun had been arranged ahead of the four remaining World Cup qualifiers that autumn. Northern Ireland's qualifying hopes had long since evaporated. But the IFA was anxious to try and get some confidence back into the squad, following demoralising defeats against England and Germany and to a lesser extent a 1-0 reversal in Poland. The trip seemed to be serving its purpose when Northern Ireland took the lead after just nine minutes. Damien Johnston was the architect with a delicate chip to the back post. David had not become Northern Ireland's leading scorer in record time by spurning opportunities like that. He leapt to head home and Northern Ireland scented a sweet success in the sun. Sadly all the goal did was make the Maltese cross. They stubbornly hauled themselves off the floor and back into the game. Ivan Woods levelled after 35 minutes and the home side were unfortunate not to win the game, when they had a last-minute penalty saved by Maik Taylor.

Left: David is pictured in action here in the Ta'Qali stadium as he is about to nutmeg Malta's Claude Mattocks. He produced a lively performance which was one of the few bright spots in an otherwise disappointing show. But in a perverse sense the way that game unfolded had a galvanising effect on the Northern Ireland players. Their frustration at drawing, indeed almost losing, a game they knew they had been quite capable of winning irritated them. After heading the opening goal Healy almost made it 2-0 with a wickedly struck free-kick before the home side got into their stride. Ivan Woods levelled things 10 minutes before the break. But he did not see the game out: he and Keith Gillespie received red cards after a poor tackle by the Northern Ireland man on Andrew Cohen. Total embarrassment was only avoided when Maik Taylor saved a last-minute penalty after Stephen Craigan upended Antoine Zahra. So no sign of the hoped-for victory, stretching Northern Ireland's run to nine games without a win.

Above: Three weeks after the debacle in Malta the Northern Ireland team trotted out at Windsor Park to face Azerbaijan. It was another potential banana skin, not helped by the public perception that as little was known about the visitors they could not be any good. But as the green and white army sang happily during the pre-match build-up at a sun-kissed national stadium, there was a feeling of optimism that it could be Northern Ireland's day. So it proved. A 2-0 victory gave the home side its first win in a competitive game for four years. After James Quinn, Stuart Elliott, Steve Davis and Stephen Craigan came close, Northern Ireland approached the hour mark becoming increasingly anxious. Then on 60 minutes Elliott fired the home side in front from a free-kick after Damien Johnston had been fouled. The sense of relief could be felt around the ground. David, pictured here battling with Zaur Tagizade, had put in a good shift despite coming in for some rough treatment from the Azerbaijan defence. With eleven minutes remaining he was replaced by the fresh legs of Steve Jones. Five minutes later Northern Ireland got a penalty. Healy, the regular penalty taker, had been deprived of the opportunity of another goal for his country by his substitution. Elliott was set to step forward to take the spot kick and claim his second goal of the day but Warren Feeney took the ball off him. He squeezed it past the Azerbaijan keeper Kramarenko to seal a 2-0 win. Next up another game in Belfast against England.

Above: The win over Azerbaijan had lifted the spirits of the entire Northern Ireland squad ahead of the home game with England on 7 September 2005. David is pictured here training with some team-mates at Newforge on the Monday before the match. England, who had walloped Northern Ireland 4-0 at Old Trafford in their home game, arrived the following day. They booked out an entire hotel – entry would have been easier to Long Kesh at the height of the Troubles – and closeted themselves away. Mr Beckham and his pals were in residence in 'our wee country', seen as a mere staging post to the 2006 World Cup – a tournament where England's golden generation believed they could win the trophy for the first time since that oft-referred-to day in July 1966. Northern Ireland were seen as bit-part players as Sven-Göran Eriksson's side moved towards what surely was their destiny. But Lord Snooty and his pals were in for a shock. The home crowd was in carnival mood. The atmosphere was electric as Northern Ireland produced the sort of do or die performance that was a throwback to the days of the Billy Bingham era. The only goal of the game came after 74 minutes. It inscribed the name of David Healy into the folklore of Northern Ireland life for ever.

Above: Wherever David Healy goes for the rest of his life someone will always want to ask him about 'that goal'. It was the 19th of his Northern Ireland career. It also sparked the sort of manic celebrations that eclipsed anything previously seen at Windsor Park. Mind you it was Northern Ireland's first home victory over England since 1927. Even Sven was not around then! David held his run, staying on-side, until a perfectly weighted ball from Steve Davis put him in. Ashley Cole could only look on in horror as the Killyleagh kid smashed his shot past a bemused Paul Robinson. Instantly the green and white army began their 'Away In A Manger' anthem about their hero.

"The stars in the bright sky look down on He-lay" was the oft-repeated cry. Simultaneously the entire Alex Russell stand behind where the goal was scored bowed their hands and heads in 'we are not worthy' stance. David Healy was now a *bona fide* legend.

Right: Although some England players could have been accused of being less than gracious after Northern Ireland's famous 1-0 win, David Beckham was not one of them. The then-Real Madrid player congratulated any Northern Ireland player who came near him with a handshake. But his exchange with Healy had particular warmth, a throwback to their days together at Manchester United. Beckham's sporting behaviour was appreciated by the Northern Ireland faithful – the same folk who had given him almost as torrid a time as their team during the 90 minutes. Despite being gutted at losing the game, Beckham has not become the icon he is without being able to see the bigger picture. He knew that while England may have lost the battle in Belfast in real terms they had already won the war. From their point of view this would come to be seen as a blip on the way to inevitable qualification for the 2006 World Cup. For Northern Ireland it was simply one of the most memorable nights in the history of football here. It was *that* special, with Healy the hero of heroes.

50   DAVID HEALY

Left: The 1-0 victory over England sparked the sort of post-match celebrations that can only be understood by people who live in Northern Ireland and support the team. The fans were ecstatic and simply refused to go home after the match. The players took a deserved lap of honour. They were cheered to the echo every inch of the way. The fans threw scarves and hats onto the pitch which the players picked up. They left the playing arena festooned in green and white Northern Ireland memorabilia. Most of the 13,500 crowd remained. Healy the hero is pictured leaving the pitch but he would return with his colleagues to allow the fans one final, climactic moment of celebration. The supporters were singing all their favourite anthems from 'Sweet Caroline' to the Healy-inspired rework of 'Away In A Manger'. Then of course there was the *pièce de résistance*: 'We're Not Brazil, We're Northern Ireland'. It was a great night to be a Northern Ireland fan in Belfast. But as comedian Patrick Kielty has since recounted, it was an even better night to be a Northern Ireland fan living in London!

Above: Are David and Keith Gillespie auditioning for 'Celebrity Come Dancing'? Or are they doing the hokey cokey, is that what it's all about? Well no actually. The pair are involved in some serious stretching during the warm-up for a training session ahead of Northern Ireland's final World Cup qualifier against Austria in October 2005. The game was played at the Ernst Happel Stadium in Vienna and ended in a 2-0 defeat. It was a disappointing end to what had been a rollercoaster campaign. It will always be remembered, of course, for that dramatic 1-0 win over England in Belfast. What tends to be forgotten though is that rather than building on that success, both the remaining games against Wales and Austria brought defeats.

Right: Despite the fact that neither side was within a bagel's jowl of qualifying for the 2006 World Cup, this final qualifying game with Austria turned out to be quite feisty. In our photograph it is plain to see that Austrian defender Martin Stranzi is not worried about making a high challenge as he and David attempt to win the ball. But the game in Vienna was especially disappointing because Northern Ireland should have gone in leading at the break. Healy, Keith Gillespie and Michael Duff all might have scored before the Austrians nicked a crucial goal from Rene Aufhauser just before the break. Despite the best efforts of Northern Ireland an equaliser failed to materialise, and then in added time Aufhauser nabbed his second. That added insult to injury after Damien Johnston's red card on 77 minutes. But at least Northern Ireland finished ahead of Wales and Azerbaijan.

Left: Having completed an unsuccessful World Cup qualifying campaign in October 2005 it was back to the shifting sands of Leeds United for David. He is pictured scoring the first goal for Leeds against Burnley in a Coca-Cola championship game at Elland Road. November had brought the news that an American consortium was interested in taking over cash-strapped Leeds. Representatives of the group had travelled from the States for this game and when Leeds went in front in the opening minute their stock was on the rise. Sadly, just like the Americans in the end, this proved to be another false dawn. Burnley levelled after 10 minutes and were ahead by the half-hour mark. The 27,000 diehards who had turned out to see the former Premiership giants drop to 17th in the Coca-Cola championship with another home defeat were gutted. They treated their American visitors to some profane singing delivered in a typically blunt Yorkshire way. Suffice to say the visitors were curious about what was going on.

Right: Football, as Jimmy Greaves once famously suggested "is a funny old game". The line between success and failure, glory and grief can be paper-thin. This picture, taken at an FA Cup replay on 17 January 2006, shows just that. Proving that the agony and the ecstasy can both be part of any game, David is seen here experiencing the downside of life as a striker. Earlier he had scored twice against Wigan at Elland Road but when the game was log-jammed at 3-3 after extra time it was down to sudden death and spot kicks. In keeping with what David will look back on as a frustrating season with Leeds, that penalty shoot-out was lost 4-3 and their FA Cup story was over. Healy had made a flying start to the season with two goals in his opening game. That plus his increasing stature at international level led to strong rumours that a move to West Ham was imminent. When Leeds signed Richard Cresswell from Healy's old club Preston the rumour mill went into overdrive. But in the end no move materialised and he finished the season at Leeds as top scorer with 14 goals. The move to London and the Premiership was to come later.

Right: This early season Yorkshire derby at Sheffield Wednesday gave Leeds the opportunity to not only get a win but also secure local bragging rights. In the end it turned out to be a 1-0 away win courtesy of a penalty. In the event it was a case of two keepers. Brad Jones had begun the match between the sticks for Wednesday. As Healy cut into the box he was challenged by Jones and took the ball past him. The keeper caught his trailing leg and the Northern Ireland international ended up in a heap in the box. Jones was sent for an early bath as the last man, a substitute keeper was pressed into service and his first act was to face David's penalty. His second was to pick the ball out of the net. The goal was enough to win the game, making it a pleasant drive home for Healy and his team-mates. Pleased as the fans were, they had other concerns as the end of the transfer window loomed. The possibility of losing Healy and Matthew Kilgallon was their worst fear. It came and went. Both players stayed and the warnings of Ken Bates that no money was available to bring in any fresh faces were greeted as par for the course by the Leeds fans.

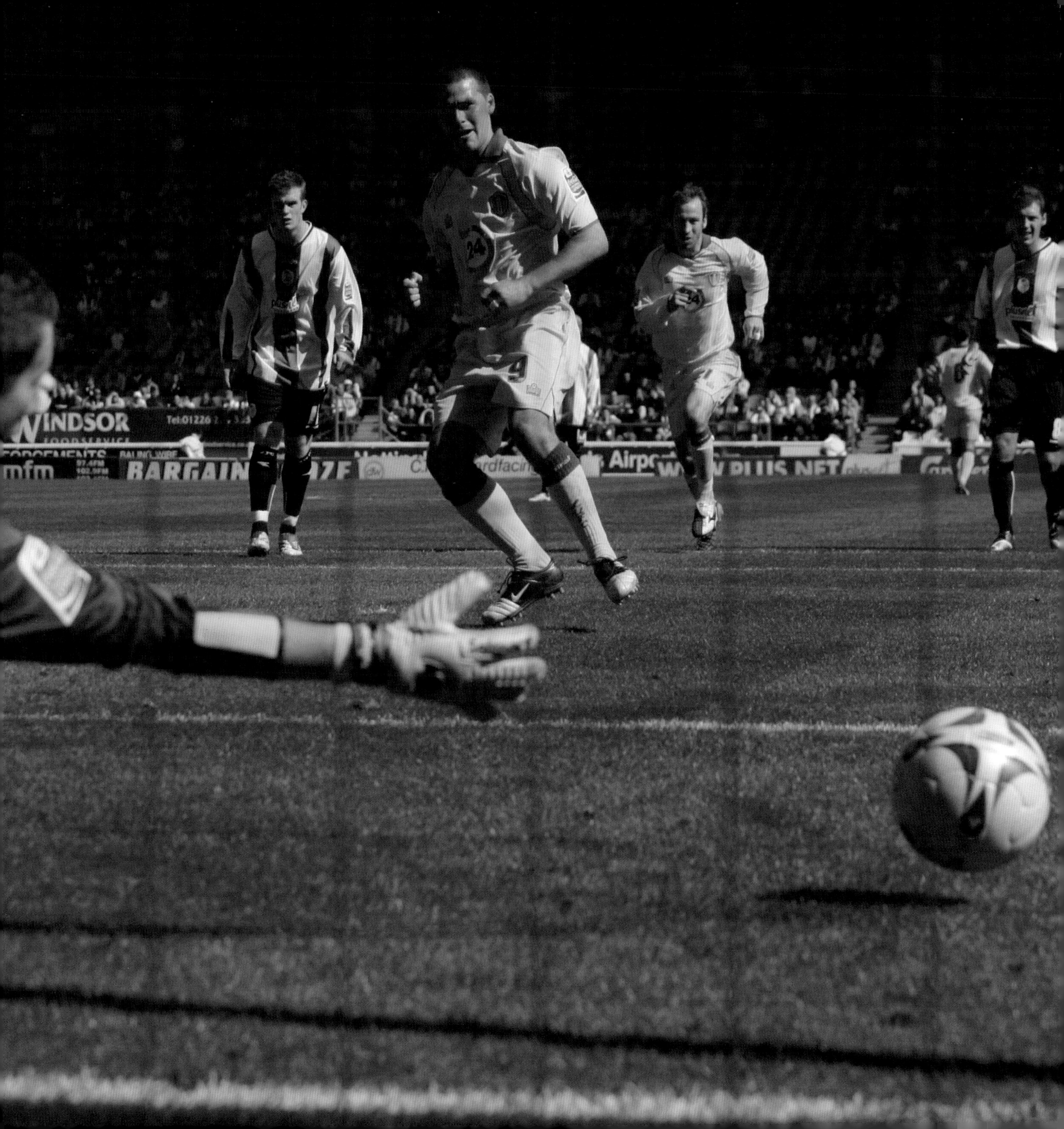
WINDSOR
BARGAIN

Above: This picture of David was snapped at Windsor Park during a Euro 2008 qualifier with Iceland. If his winner against England or his hat trick against Spain produced Healy's sweetest memories of playing for his country at Windsor Park, the 3-0 defeat by Iceland must rank as his sourest. Not that he personally had an especially bad day. Indeed he even had the ball in the net, only for it to be disallowed for offside. But the side's performance in the opening 45 was such that even the usually sympathetic home crowd booed them off. Nobody was more shocked by this than the then-manager Lawrie Sanchez. Nor indeed was anyone more responsible. It had become evident from early on that Eidur Gudjohnsen was getting far too much room in the middle of the park. He was dominating the game. No FIFA coaching badges or lap-top PowerPoint presentations were needed to realise this. Nor was membership of MENSA. It was as plain as night follows day. By the time Sanchez had closed the gate the horse had already bolted. But that bitterest of disappointments was followed by supreme joy the following Wednesday. Inevitably David would be the man who made it happen.

Right: David is pictured here celebrating with Keith Gillespie, his greatest buddy in the Northern Ireland camp. Their delight came after Healy had scored against Spain at Windsor Park. His hat-trick that evening produced the greatest win by a Northern Ireland side in living memory. Even greater than the victory in the 1982 World Cup in Spain, epic as that was with ten men, because the boys in green twice came from behind to win it. The euphoric fans refused to leave the ground after the game and stayed singing and partying until they got another glimpse of their heroes. Sadly some of the gloss was taken off the victory by the selfish antics of manager Lawrie Sanchez after the match. He threw his coat into the crowd which some construed as a farewell gift after he refused to attend the post-match press conference. Inevitably the next morning's headlines were dominated by Sanchez, when they should all have been about the team and Healy's hat-trick. Sanchez allegedly threatened to resign but stayed on for a few more matches before jumping ship and joining Fulham, leaving Northern Ireland without a manager half-way through their Euro 2008 qualifying campaign.

Above: As David Healy left the pitch after scoring a hat-trick against a formidable Spanish side he was encouraged by the scrum of photographers to raise three fingers. To make his treble even sweeter, Northern Ireland had twice come from behind to win against a Spanish side packed with top calibre players like Casillas, Alonso, Fabregas and Villa. For the record Healy's first came when he swivelled to turn in Kyle Lafferty's nod down and equalise Xabi Alonso's opener. The second, which came after David Villa had restored Spain's lead, was swept in from a Sammy Clingan free-kick – and so to the winner. The third came from a long Maik Taylor clearance which the Spanish defence failed to deal with, and David ran in and lobbed Iker Casillas as he raced from goal. After the disappointment of the Iceland defeat this win breathed new life into the quest for Euro 2008 qualification. It was a greater achievement than beating England a year earlier.

Right: In September Leeds had just sacked manager Kevin Blackwell and languished in the bottom three of the Championship table. John Carver was made caretaker manager and Birmingham City were his first opponents. A crowd of just 19,000 was paltry by the normal standards at Elland Road. Especially for a game with Birmingham City, one of the pace setters in that season's Championship. David is pictured here celebrating the first of his two goals. Healy scored twice in the opening half, the second being a penalty. However Birmingham twice came back, despite having Northern Ireland's Damien Johnston sent off. With the game evenly poised at 2-2; enter Birmingham City's Oliver Tebily. As Steve Stone stretched to try and direct a cross goalwards Tebily beat him to it. Sadly for the Frenchman he also deceived City keeper Maik Taylor; his own-goal gave Leeds three points and moved them out of the bottom three.

Above: Northern Ireland travelled to Denmark in fine fettle in October 2006 following that dramatic win over Spain in Belfast. David's hat-trick had allowed him to emulate one of his heroes, the greatest of them all George Best. Bestie had been the last Northern Ireland player to notch a hat-trick at Windsor Park. That was in a World Cup qualifier against Cyprus in the spring of 1971. Amazingly the last Northern Ireland hat-trick before Healy's treble against Spain had been scored 15 years to the day of the game with the Spanish. That was by Colin Clarke against the Faroe Islands. Our picture shows David with Liverpool's Danny Agger in close attendance in the Euro 2008 qualifier. The game ended scoreless, so David would have to wait a little longer to extend his goals tally for his country.

Right: Healy's wait for another Northern Ireland goal lasted all of four days! It came in the next Euro 2008 qualifier at Windsor Park against Latvia. The goal, which came 10 minutes before the end of the first half, gave a snapshot of David the consummate goal-scoring opportunist. As Keith Gillespie picked him out with a carefully flighted ball, Healy cleverly headed over the oncoming Latvian defender. That gave him a free run on goal and as the visiting keeper rushed towards him 'King David' coolly slotted the ball past him. It was a clinical finish to a move of panache and invention and also Healy's fourth goal in three games. Here was a striker brimming with confidence and operating at the peak of his powers. Could it really get any better than this? We didn't know the half of it...

Above: David is pictured leaving the Windsor Park pitch with Maik Taylor, a regular adversary at club level, following a 1-0 win over Latvia in October 2006. Healy had outsmarted Maris Smirnovs before knocking the ball past Aleksandrs Kolinko to score the only goal of the game. Obviously Northern Ireland would have loved a second but despite the best efforts of Kyle Lafferty, Keith Gillespie and Jonny Evans it stayed 1-0. That always gives the opposition a chance because history suggests they will always get at least one chance in the game. So it proved after 73 minutes when Girts Karlsons seemed poised to score. But Taylor made a magnificent block to save his shot and Evans completed the clearance. So the ace shot stopper had joined the ace goal scorer as heroes of the hour. It also gave Northern Ireland an impressive run of six wins, one draw and three defeats in their last 10 games.

Right: David is pictured here with Lawrie Sanchez, his current club boss at Fulham and also the man who allowed his international career to come to the boil. It was during the Euro 2008 qualifier with Latvia in Belfast. Although given his international debut by Sammy McIlroy, Healy never really flourished under the Espana '82 hero, whose preoccupation with a 4-5-1 formation left the lone striker with a thankless task and few chances. In his 29 internationals prior to the arrival of Sanchez David had scored just eight goals. During the former Wimbledon star's tenure as Northern Ireland manager he managed 20 in 27 games. By any standards that is a phenomenal record. Sanchez deserves credit for trying to ease Healy's burden by giving him a big partner to play off, generally James Quinn or Kyle Lafferty. He also ensured that during his tenure the ratio of crosses into the box was upped considerably. That was playing to David's strengths and would make him ultimately the team's greatest strength.

Above: David went into this game with Sweden on the back of a hot scoring streak. His seven goals thus far had taken him to the top of the Euro 2008 qualifiers scoring chart. That was unheard of for a Northern Ireland striker, but then when it comes to representing his country Healy seems to be able to find an extra gear. The table-topping Swedes rolled into Belfast at the top of Group F. Within 26 minutes they had silenced the home crowd by taking the lead. But then six minutes later Sweden failed to deal with a long ball into the box by Aaron Hughes. Healy said 'thank you very much' and volleyed the loose ball over the bemused Swedish keeper Isaksson. Healy is pictured here after scoring. The crowd immediately began to sing its 'Away In A Manger' song about him. But as Jimmy Cricket used to say – "there's more"! Near the hour mark Damien Johnston made a surge down the right. He whipped over a cross which Healy delicately nudged past the keeper to win the game 2-1. It brought his total in the qualifying campaign to an amazing nine goals and put Northern Ireland top of the group at the halfway stage of the qualifying campaign. Everything in the garden was rosy, but suddenly the rug was pulled away by Messrs Sanchez and Al Fayed.

Right: After scoring 'that goal' against England in September 2005 David became a football icon to the Northern Ireland public. But 13 months later a hat-trick against Spain copper-fastened the whole thing. He had moved from back to front page news! Being a celebrity is something quite different from being well known. Well-known people are recognised and often asked for their autograph. Celebrities are pursued by the paparazzi. Their autograph is demanded. Their lives to a greater or lesser degree are often not their own. Take George Best for example. If he had gone into Belfast to buy a shirt any time after the age of 17 a 10-minute job could have taken half a day. David is not quite in that position but if he went shopping in Belfast he would soon be under siege from fans. The upside of this sort of celebrity is that it opens up commercial opportunities. David is pictured here turning on the Christmas lights in Belfast in November 2006. Next to him is Liz McLarnon, famous for being in Atomic Kitten. Next to her is Calum Best, famous for being George's son.

Left: David is pictured tackling Estonia's Urmas Rooba during the friendly international at Windsor Park in March 2006. It was the first of two warm-up games ahead of the Euro 2008 qualifiers the following autumn. However with regard to this game the term 'warm up' was something of a misnomer as it began to snow during the second half! That gave the crowd the opportunity to sing their way through a selection of songs appropriate to the inclement weather. It also gave Northern Ireland the opportunity to blood some fringe strikers like Peter Thompson of Linfield and Steve Jones of the eccentric hair-cut. That meant David went off for a warm bath as the game approached the hour mark. He did not score on the night, but did flick on James Quinn's cross for debut boy Ivan Sproule to score after a mere 77 seconds! That was Northern Ireland's quickest since Danny Wilson's effort after 56 seconds in the late '80s against Poland. It was also the first win by the boys in green in a friendly match at home in eight years.

Above: Liechtenstein have been regular opponents of Northern Ireland in recent years. However when we relieved them of their record as the European country who went longest without scoring, nobody was feeling too pleased. So when they came out of the hat for the Euro 2008 qualifiers Northern Ireland determined to put on a good show. The first game was an away match which was won 4-1 with David creating another bit of history. He became the first Northern Ireland player ever to score two hat-tricks, following up his treble against Spain in Belfast with another triple strike in Vaduz. These goals took Healy's international tally to 27 goals in his 55 appearances for his country. His second hat-trick had manager Lawrie Sanchez drooling. "David is a world class finisher. We play to his strengths and he rewards us all the time," admitted the Northern Ireland boss. "David is our fulcrum: the player everybody talks about. But without the other players doing their jobs we would not be winning matches."

Right: David is pictured here running off to celebrate the second goal of his three against Liechtenstein in Vaduz. Perhaps he scented the fact that he was possibly on another hat-trick and this could be adding to his joy! The goal came with a quarter of an hour of the match remaining. Keith Gillespie was again the provider with a killer through-ball. With the smell of a goal in his nostrils, Healy left two defenders for dead and placed the ball past Peter Jehle, the home keeper, as instinctively as a dog barks at the postman. That made the score 2-0. Eight minutes later David had bagged that hat-trick, his current Fulham club-mate Steve Davis being the provider on this occasion. Franz Burgmeier ruined Maik Taylor's hopes of a clean sheet by curling in a consolation goal on 90 minutes. But Northern Ireland hit them where it hurts in added time when Grant McCann rose to head home another pinpoint delivery from Gillespie and make it 4-1. A good night's work overall and another milestone in David's unbelievable scoring odyssey.

DAVID HEALY

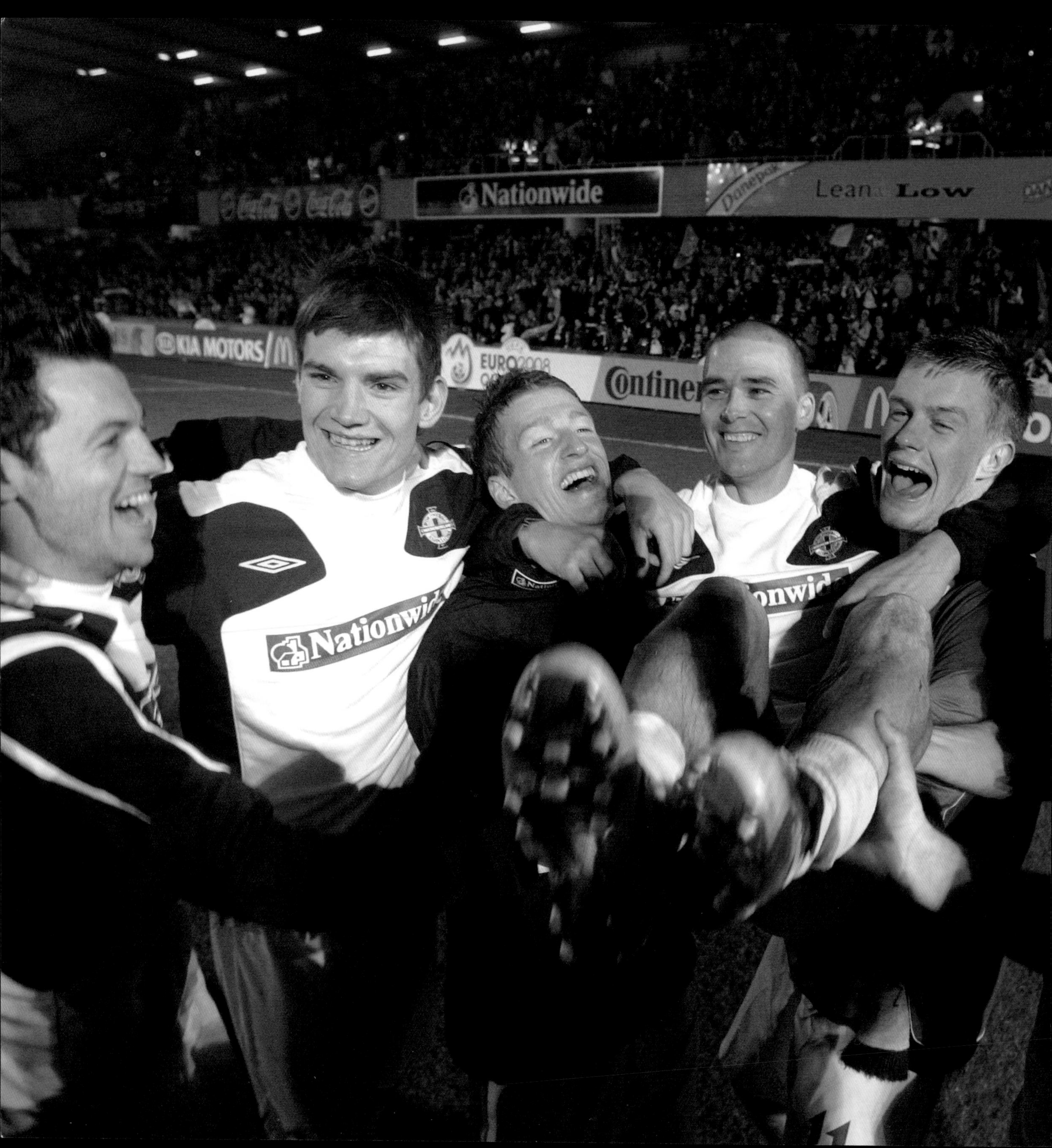
Nationwide
KIA MOTORS
EURO2008
Nationwide

Left: Healy's two-goal blast against the Swedes ensured he stayed ahead of the German international Lukas Podolski. Given the German nation's standing and record in world soccer this was literally David and Goliath stuff! Lawrie Sanchez, in what was to be his last game in charge of Northern Ireland, had guided his team to the top of Group F. Admittedly he had done so without having to face tricky away games in Sweden and Spain, but nobody could take away the fact that he had done it. He was smart enough to know the job was far from over, with four of the last six matches away from home. A good time to leave? Perhaps. But he did strike a cautionary note after the win over the Swedes. "There is a lot of football still to be played in this group," rapped Sanchez. How prophetic that proved to be. However on the night of 28 March 2007 nobody in the Windsor Park stands was listening. They all wanted to party. The team knew that and showed their appreciation to the fans by holding Healy aloft for them. Everyone savoured the moment, none of them knowing that by the time the next match came around Sanchez would have flown the coop and been replaced by Nigel Worthington, David's old boss at Norwich.

Above: Sweden were top of the Euro 2008 qualifying group, had players from the top leagues around Europe and a habit for qualifying for major finals when they jetted into Belfast in March 2007. Yet Northern Ireland were full of confidence, due to the extraordinary goal scoring feats of 'King David' Healy. The game began and suddenly after 27 minutes it all went pear-shaped. The Swedes, having absorbed some early pressure, went in front through Johan Elmander. He held off a challenge from Aaron Hughes before placing his shot beyond Maik Taylor. But four minutes later David had the home faithful dancing around Windsor. He took aim from 18 yards and unloaded a dipping shot past the astonished Andreas Isaksson. He is seen here celebrating with strike partner Warren Feeney after scoring. Feeney is an interesting character, being the third generation of his family to don the green jersey. His grandfather Jimmy was the first, followed by his Dad Warren and now junior makes three! For Healy that night the magic number was 'two'. He completed his double for the evening after 59 minutes. Damien Johnston's superb run and low cross to the near post was almost nonchalantly flicked home to win the game. When Healy left the pitch near the end he was given a standing ovation after notching his ninth goal of the qualifying campaign.

Left: When Northern Ireland travelled to Latvia on the fir
weekend of September 2007 hopes were high that the on
seemingly impossible dream of Euro 2008 could start to becom
a reality. Latvia on the Saturday would be followed by Iceland th
following Wednesday. Even four points out of six would have t
boys in green sitting pretty and the fans ringing their travel agen
But when early pressure failed to yield a goal the Latvians began
get more confident. Keith Gillespie and a couple of efforts fro
David failed to trouble the home keeper Andris Vannis. Thin
went from bad to worse soon after the break when a Chris Bai
own-goal edged Latvia in front. Northern Ireland were chasi
the game and as our picture shows the home defence were taki
no prisoners. Tripping Healy is clearly not enough for Dzinta
Zirnis. He adds insult to injury by elbowing him in the bac
A Kyle Lafferty effort, a header from David, a couple of Chr
Brunt long range efforts and a close range header from Jonn
Evans failed to bring an equaliser. A 1-0 defeat was a sorry end
a day that had begun so optimistically.

Right: After the disaster in Latvia, Northern Ireland travelled to Iceland. There was a feeling within the squad that they owed Iceland one following the shambolic opening game of the qualifying campaign when they had beaten Northern Ireland 3-0 in Belfast. However the home side took an early lead and held it until 72 minutes. Then Kari Arnason brought down Healy in the box on 72 minutes. 'King David' dusted himself down and fired home the resulting penalty. It was goal number 12 of the qualifying campaign, equalling the record set by Davor Suker of Croatia ahead of Euro 1996. A win would have taken Northern Ireland to the top of their group. But a point was a point: the guys would take it and move on. Then right at the death disaster struck. Keith Gillespie was dealt a cruel blow when he inadvertently turned Gretar Steinson's cross into his own net. Our picture shows an understandably unhappy Keith berating team-mates Michael Duff, Steve Davis and even his buddy Healy. The odds of Northern Ireland losing both games may well have been long. But the odds against them doing it by two own goals were longer still. With three games to go were Northern Ireland out of it?

Right: After the desolation of two defeats on the bounce against Latvia and Iceland, Northern Ireland faced another away game in Sweden. Pre-match media talk was all about how the Swedes always seem to qualify for all major finals, how many of their players perform in the top leagues around Europe. Northern Ireland were on a tanking it seemed. When Olof Mellberg edged Sweden in front early on, the portents looked far from good. Apart from anything else it was a poor goal defensively to concede. With confidence already in a fragile state and several key players missing through injury and suspension, everyone wondered if this was going to be a damage limitation exercise. But Nigel Worthington's boys stuck to his game plan. They took on board his advice and confounded the critics by snatching a second-half equaliser from Kyle Lafferty. In our picture the big Burnley youngster is snapped in the act of scoring as David looks on. Many felt he should have passed to Healy just before this – thank goodness he chose not to!

Right: David is pictured here grappling for possession with Olof Mellberg during the Sweden/Northern Ireland Group F Euro 2008 qualifier on 17 October 2007. The pair are Premiership adversaries when Fulham play Aston Villa, but on this occasion the Swedes were attempting to exact revenge for a surprise defeat in Belfast the previous March. On that occasion Healy was the tormentor-in-chief with his two goals securing the points after Sweden had gone in front. So when Northern Ireland arrived for the game the Swedish media had already identified David as the danger man. Some went to extremes, mind you. One particular publication printed a picture of Healy's head superimposed on a sheep, clearing indicating that he would not pull the wool over their eyes a second time!

Right: What a joyous sight! Northern Ireland players celebrate with Kyle Lafferty after he had equalised against Sweden in the Rasunda Stadium. The goal tied the game up at 1-1 and that is how it finished. This precious point meant that Northern Ireland went into their final qualifying games in Group F knowing that, mathematically at least, they could still qualify for Euro 2008. On the night Lafferty really showed that even though he had just turned 20 he was rapidly coming of age as an international player. His physical presence, hard running and aerial threat make him the perfect foil for the more diminutive Healy. Northern Ireland fans are hoping that their striking partnership can continue to blossom in coming seasons. Where that will be in terms of home games, remains to be seen. If Windsor Park's capacity is further reduced by the Health & Safety mandarins, the IFA have indicated that playing there would no longer be viable. With any new stadium being a minimum of three years away at least, or so we are told, that would be a pity. So could the game with Denmark be the last senior international to be played at Windsor Park?

DAVID ON BEING 'HEA-LAY'!

Deputy First Minster Martin McGuinness is quick to speak out when he believes any of his fellow politicians "lose the run of themselves". Nobody could ever accuse David Healy of that. One of his most endearing qualities is his refusal to get carried away by his own success.

"I just want to put away the chances I am presented with. That is my job," reasons David. "It is an honour to play for Northern Ireland. But to be known as your country's top goal scorer is something else."

Getting that goal-scoring record always seemed a possibility once David scored twice on his debut against Luxembourg at the tender age of 20. But then very often in football things do not go according to plan. Take Norman Whiteside as an example.

When he became the youngest player ever to appear in a World Cup at 17 years and 41 days, eclipsing the great Brazilian Pele, it was assumed he would go on to become his country's all-time top scorer. In the end 'Big Norm' managed nine goals in 28 games for his country. He recalls that himself and Gerry Armstrong were always "busting to get into double figures".

David equalled Norman's nine goals for Northern Ireland with that golden goal that ended what he describes as "the barren spell", when the boys in green went 1,298 minutes without scoring. That was against Norway in February 2004. The following month he got into double figures with the winner against Estonia. Since then he simply cannot stop scoring, and on reaching his 60th cap against Sweden in October 2007 he had amassed an amazing 32 goals.

Gerry Armstrong always believed that the national scoring record would ultimately be captured by David. It was jointly held by Billy Gillespie, who played in the 1920s, and Colin Clarke who equalled it some 15 years before Healy came on the scene.

"But he has surprised even me in terms of goals," laughs big Gerry, immortalised by that winning goal against Spain at Espana

'82. "Initially I suggested he would get over 20. Already he has managed more than 30 and he has his best years ahead of him hopefully." Big Gerry, who scored a dozen goals in 63 international appearances, was Northern Ireland's assistant manager when Healy finally equalled and then broke that goal-scoring record in a match with Trinidad & Tobago.

The first one was a 40-yard lob and the one that gave him the record a tap in from six yards. At 24 and after 35 caps Healy was Northern Ireland's most successful goal scorer ever.

"For me, the pick of them has to be the one he got against a quality England side," reckons Armstrong. So what are David's memories of 'that goal'?

"I remember closing their goalkeeper down and then getting back in late behind their defence. Steve Davis showed great composure to bring it down, wait and then play me in. It was one of those where I have sort of bent the run a bit, and somebody has played me on-side. I looked across at the linesman who had his flag down and the ball bounced for me: I hit it and fortunately for me it went in. The place erupted. There was flares. There was flags. There was people throwing scarves on to the pitch. I had scored. We were beating England at Windsor Park. The atmosphere was electric. It was truly a memorable, memorable night."

It was a night also that turned the kid from Killyleagh into front page news. But while his career was blossoming in the international arena, things were not so good at club level.

Leeds United, the so-called sleeping giant that David had joined from Preston a year previously, continued to struggle with the financial burden left by previous regimes. Many have argued, with seeming justification, that Healy was never utilised properly in his time at the club. The decision to play David on the flanks rather than through the middle mystified Northern Ireland fans.

If his success on the international stage had proven anything it was that given the correct service he could produce the goods. Nigel Worthington, who has managed him at both club and international level, sees it in very simple terms. "When he gets that ball in the box, nine times out of ten he is going to score!"

Although the going was tough at times for David, particularly in his last days at Leeds when the eccentric Ken Bates was in charge, he never despaired. He admits though that his children proved to be a great help.

"It's great to have Taylor and Jude. I suppose it is the same for every parent, that no matter how they are feeling they can always rely on their kids to cheer them up," suggests David. "If I came home from games and things hadn't gone well or I hadn't done as well as I know I can, they are always there to get you motivated to get going again."

Happily Healy got away from the increasingly claustrophobic atmosphere at Leeds when Lawrie Sanchez took him to Fulham in the summer of 2007. It was dream come true for 'King David'.

"The Premiership is the top league in the world. All the top foreign players want to play there, and I have always wanted to get back since I left Manchester United. In this league every game is a big game. But I think I can play in the Premier League. In the past some people were writing me off as an international player when we had that barren spell. I proved them wrong in the past and I can do so again."

Given his international goal-scoring pedigree, the English Premier League is clearly the place Healy deserves to be. He has been elevated to iconic status, especially in his own country, but childhood memories help keep him in touch with reality.

"I grew up as a supporter of Northern Ireland, and if I wasn't playing I would be still supporting them 100%," says David. "I went to Windsor Park as a kid with my dad, friends and family. I'm sure there would have been kids at the England game looking to me for inspiration. If there was any advice I would give them it is to keep working hard. Then hopefully I will see them in the Northern Ireland set-up in a couple of years. The thing about sport is that the impossible is possible as we proved the night we beat England. Teams win games - not individuals. England had far better individuals than us that night. But I think we outworked them as a team, and I think we also outworked them as individuals. They never once outclassed us as they should have done and as they were expected to do. We went out with a great team spirit - as we always do for Northern Ireland - and in the end I think we got a deserved win."

On that particular occasion Sanchez has subsequently admitted that he had a game plan that he thought could rattle England. It was to turn the game into the sort of frenetic match you often get in the Championship, the level immediately below the Premier League.

The other thing he encouraged his side to do was to make Rio Ferdinand head the ball as often as possible - the rationale here being that he was always at his most comfortable when the ball was on the deck. Rio and his big name colleagues like Wayne Rooney, Frank Lampard, David Beckham *et al* were anything but comfortable that September evening in Belfast.

Amazingly though 'that goal' as it has become known is not really Healy's personal highlight amongst his scoring exploits for Northern Ireland. "The goal I probably remember most was my first at Windsor Park against the then-Yugoslavia. It was very special and made me believe that I could score at international level."

That particular goal came in a 2-1 friendly defeat at Windsor Park in August 2000. Jeff Whitley slid a defence-splitting pass through to David, who showed the ice-cool composure for which he is now famous, by cheekily pushing the ball through the advancing keeper's legs.

Surprisingly David does not rate the win over England or even his hat-trick game against Spain in September 2006 as Northern Ireland's top performance in his time. "In recent years we have had victories against England and Spain and even Sweden in Belfast. But I would say the 1-1 draw in the away game with the Swedes was one of the best all-round performances since I have been playing international football. We passed the ball better than them. We moved it better than them and we looked the stronger and fitter team as the game wore on. Sweden's record at home is fantastic, but we outplayed them on the night. It is not often we go away from home and are the better side against one of the strongest nations in Europe. I really believe we should have won."

After that game the blues of the defeats on the road trips to Latvia and Iceland were banished. Healy chose that moment to speak up for Nigel Worthington. "Some people blamed him for those defeats but the players to a man knew they had let both him and themselves down. There comes a time when the players have to hold their hands up. Nigel took over at a difficult time when Lawrie left, and he is doing a great job. I have worked with him before and we know each other's strengths. Obviously it is up to him and the IFA, but I would like to see him stay after his six game contract is completed."

As David settles down to life in the Premier League does he ever wonder about what might have been, had he stayed at Old Trafford? "I have no regrets about leaving to join Preston six years ago. I knew I was going to be fifth – maybe sixth – choice for the first team, and I needed regular first team football to protect my Northern Ireland place. I talked it over with Sir Alex Ferguson who was always good to me. He let me know his views and wanted to know mine. There were no hard feelings. Everyone wants to play for Manchester United whether it's once or a hundred times. I will never forget my debut in front of 67,000 at Old Trafford. But to have been part of that Manchester United set-up from such a young age – I was 12 or 13 – to get to meet the manager and the top players was fantastic. Then to be invited to go there at 16. The opportunity, the coaching, the lifestyle was everything any boy could want. So I have no regrets."

The man who winkled David away from Old Trafford to Preston was the current Everton manager David Moyes, then making a name for himself at Deepdale. "David Healy was a big signing for me at the time," remembers Moyes. "He scored 10 goals in 20 games which got me to the play-off final. I am pleased he is now playing in the Premiership. I'm sure he'll score goals but hopefully not against Everton!"

Whatever lies ahead for David in his club career, his exploits in the green jersey of Northern Ireland to date have ensured that he will always have a special place in the hearts of the fans. Those trademark goals ensure that. But there is also the fact that the Northern Ireland supporters look on Healy as one of their own. He is living out the dream of everyone in the crowd: the fan who got on to the pitch and did the business.

David makes no secret of the pride he gets out of representing his country. "Everybody knows how proud I am to play for Northern Ireland," ventures David. "At first I wanted to consolidate my place, and then I wanted to reach that elusive figure of 13 goals. It seemed like a long haul at the time but I got there. After that I wanted to go on and score more goals for my country and possibly set a mark."

Nobody could argue against his achievements. At present David is on course to set the bar for scoring goals for Northern Ireland so high that nobody coming after him will be able to jump it.

Only the most perverse would disagree with the assertion that Healy is the greatest natural finisher ever to don the green jersey. The fans have no doubt that 'King David' reigns supreme.

OTHERS ON HEALY

David Healy is without doubt the most iconic Northern Ireland footballer currently playing the game.

While it can be said that his scoring record at club level does not match his 'goals per game' ratio for Northern Ireland, many players would still be delighted with it. At club level he averages a goal every four games. At international level this is better than one in two. So what is his secret?

Current Northern Ireland keeper Maik Taylor reckons that while Healy makes scoring goals look ridiculously easy at times, he works at it. Indeed the harder he works the better he gets! "He is unbelievable," admits the Birmingham custodian. "But believe me, he puts the work in on the training pitch. I've have seen him stay behind after training many times. But it works for him. He is up there with the best finishers I have ever worked with."

While hard work undoubtedly plays its part, former Northern Ireland international Roy Coyle thinks there is more to it than that. "All great strikers have one big asset – anticipation," reasons the man who is the most successful manager ever in local football. "His awareness is paramount. The ball is like a magnet to him when it comes into the box. That is something certain players are born with. There is a distinct difference between people who score goals and goal-scorers. But David is like a predator in the wild when he is in or around goal. For me he is undoubtedly the best finisher Northern Ireland has ever had. But then his record proves that."

From the day he pulled on a Northern Ireland jersey for the first time, David always had that 13-goal record jointly held by Billy Gillespie and Colin Clarke in his sights. He served notice in his very first game that

he could be the answer to his country's scoring problems, by bagging two goals on his debut in Luxembourg.

"Northern Ireland has always had a problem down the years scoring goals. The record books tell us that," reasons Northern Ireland manager Nigel Worthington. "But the thing about David is that when the ball drops to him in the box, nine times out of ten he will score."

Gerry Armstrong, one of the heroes of Espana '82 and now a soccer analyst on Sky, knows a player with a goal-scoring pedigree when he sees one. "I knew from day one he would score goals. But he has even exceeded my expectations," reveals big Gerry. "If I am being honest, I don't know if anyone will ever get anywhere near the tally he is going to finish up with. He has an unbelievable knack of being able to score goals out of nothing. His secret is that he has a great finish in both feet. He also has great instincts in the box – a knack of being in the right place at the right time. He is simply one of the best finishers that Northern Ireland has ever produced."
Until David scored 'that goal' against England at Windsor Park on 7 September 2005, the most talked about goal scored by Northern Ireland came from Armstrong's boot, on the night Billy Bingham's side shocked world football by beating Spain in Valencia.

Billy Hamilton played in that game. The big man is an admirer of Healy's scoring prowess, recognises his natural goal-scoring instincts but also feels the entire 1982 World Cup squad owe him a debt. "Once he scored that goal against England we all breathed a collective sigh of relief," grins big Billy. "It meant that after all this time we could finally get Gerry to stop talking about his goal against Spain!"

That 1982 squad have a camaraderie that has never been diluted by the years. When they meet up again Hamilton says they are "like brothers".

Left: David Healy scores his second goal against Leichtenstein at Windsor Park, Belfast to the despair of the opposition

But that does not stop the incessant teasing of one another. Hence the quips about Armstrong.

Another member of that august group is the former Leicester City and Norwich centre-half John O'Neill. Now back in his native Derry, big John has proven to be an able and shrewd analyst for the BBC on international football. "What can you say about David Healy? His record number of goals for Northern Ireland says it all. I sometimes wonder what we could have achieved if he had been around in Spain in 1982." Former Northern Ireland internationals are all ready to praise 'King David' for his scoring exploits. One of his former managers admits that while he is not surprised at Healy's scoring exploits, he is more impressed by the fact that he has scored so many for his country.

"His scoring record for his country is fantastic," concedes Manchester United boss Sir Alex Ferguson. "It was hard to imagine that he would go on to that level when we let him go to Preston for £1.5m when he was only young. Unfortunately his value has never increased, which is surprising, but he has got his chance in the Premier League now which is good."

Hans-Peter Zaugg, who managed Liechtenstein and witnessed David destroy them first-hand with five goals in two games, feels the Killyleagh kid is a natural, and could score goals in any company. "I believe David Healy could score goals for countries and clubs across Europe," ventures Zaugg. "Healy can seem to disappear from games, you forget he is on the field and then suddenly he gets a goal. He can score in different ways, and if he gets just one chance he rarely misses."

One of the greatest goal-scorers of modern times has been the former Liverpool and Republic of Ireland international John Aldridge. He believes the secret of being a goal-scorer is essentially down to one thing. "Goal-scoring is about confidence," opines Aldo. "Healy has it. He also has a great scoring record for Northern Ireland."

Aldridge's former Liverpool and international colleague Mark Lawrenson also believes a player who is content in his own mind does the business on the pitch. "David pulls on that green shirt of Northern Ireland and he feels comfortable and confident. He goes out there and scores goals for fun. He needs to get that same feeling at club level. If he does then there is no reason why he won't score goals in the Premiership."

Former Northern Ireland manager Sammy McIlroy was the man who plucked Healy from the outer fringes of the first team at Manchester United and gave him his debut in the green jersey. "I had no hesitation in bringing him into the Northern Ireland set-up," remembers Sammy. "I saw something in him the first time I saw him play for United Reserves. His movement in the box was great, and no matter where he got the ball he always knew exactly where the goal was."

Alan McDonald had a distinguished career at the heart of the Northern Ireland defence. He won 52 caps and has coached the Under-21 side for the past five years, a job he now combines with managing Glentoran. "I worked closely with David when I helped Sammy out with the senior side for six games," recalls Alan. "His sharpness in the box and the quality of his finishing is superb. Given half a chance he is lethal. His quickness and speed of thought is also a brilliant asset. I just think though that he has a God-given gift of knowing where the net is. Goal-scoring comes naturally to him. He has the knack of being in the right place at the right time. Alan Shearer had that, so has David. He has been a revelation in a Northern Ireland shirt, and is also one of the nicest guys you could meet. His success has not gone to his head. He is humble and always wants to turn up and play for the shirt."

McDonald's fellow Irish League manager at Lisburn Distillery Paul Kirk, one of the most colourful characters in the local game, knows a thing or two about goal-scoring. He was a free-scoring striker who has the unique distinction of winning titles with three different Belfast clubs: Glentoran, Crusaders and Linfield. His son Andrew is also a striker and has partnered Healy on a number of occasions for Northern Ireland. Kirk feels David is the real deal. "His record for Northern Ireland is absolutely unbelievable," purrs Paul. "But the gift he has is born in him. You cannot coach that. He never freezes in front of goal. He is always calculating, cool and clinical. He always seems to have time, never bottles it and hits the target."

Northern Ireland skipper Aaron Hughes, now a club colleague of Healy's at Fulham, is in no doubt about his team-mate's contribution to the Northern Ireland cause. "To have someone like David, to do what he does, is one of the reasons we have been so successful in recent times," suggests the national team's captain. "The key at international level is to take your chances when you have them. David is always a threat, we just have to get the ball to him."

Former Northern Ireland manager Lawrie Sanchez tailored his team selections to play to Healy's strengths. He tried to get players wide who would whip crosses into the box, and also liked to have a big man for David to play off. "His strike rate for Northern Ireland is ridiculous," raps the Fulham boss. "Also, he doesn't just score against the Latvias of this world. He scored against England, Germany…and then there was the hat-trick against Spain. His main strength is simple – he scores goals."

One man who would agree with that is the Everton boss David Moyes. He was in charge at Preston when he persuaded David to leave Old Trafford and advance his career with first team football at Deepdale. "We went very close, with David in the team, to getting into the Premier League with Preston. His 10 goals in 20 games after I signed him were a major factor in getting us to the play-offs. He did great for me really. He comes from a good family and is a nice lad. I'm sure that he will do well in the Premier League, and I'm pleased for him that he has done so well in his career to date."

Dr Malcolm Brodie, doyen of football journalism in Northern Ireland for almost sixty years, has seen a lot of strikers come and go in his time. He believes Healy is a class apart. "He was a breath of fresh air when he came into the Northern Ireland set-up," muses Malcolm. "He is unquestionably a quality player. Indeed, I would go so far as to say that he is undoubtedly the most naturally gifted goal-scorer that Northern Ireland has ever had."

For the final word on 'King David' we return to Nigel Worthington, the first man to have managed Healy at club and then international level. "One of the things that makes David special is his attitude to the game. He still wants to learn," notes Nigel. "He is not one of those players who requires to be driven to be successful. David drives himself. As a finisher I would sum him up in one word – lethal! Quite simply, that's what he is all about."

ACKNOWLEDGEMENTS

The publisher wishes to thank the following for permission to reproduce work in copyright

© PAPhotos.com (pp. 9, 10, 14, 18, 19, 23, 26-27, 28, 29, 30, 31, 32, 33, 35, 36, 38-39, 40-41, 42, 45, 46, 47, 48, 49, 50-51, 52-53, 54, 55, 62, 63, 64, 66, 67, 68, 69, 70, 71, 72, 73, 74-75, 76, 77, 78-79, 80-81, 82-83, 84-85, 86-87, 88, 92)

© actionimages.com (pp. 20-21, 22, 24, 25, 34, 37, 43, 56-57, 58-59, 60-61, 65)

© Conor McCaughley (pp. 16, 17, 44)